SIDEBROW BOOKS

LETTERS TO KELLY CLARKSON

Published by Sidebrow Books
P.O. Box 170113
San Francisco, CA 94117-0113
sidebrow@sidebrow.net
www.sidebrow.net

Cover art by Laura Splan ("Wallpaper," 2008, blood on wallpaper)
Cover & book design by Jason Snyder

ISBN: 0-9814975-6-X
ISBN-13: 978-0-9814975-6-3

FIRST EDITION | FIRST PRINTING
9 8 7 6 5 4 3 2 1
SIDEBROW BOOKS 007
PRINTED IN THE UNITED STATES

Sidebrow Books titles are distributed by
Small Press Distribution

Titles are available directly from Sidebrow at
www.sidebrow.net/books

A Member of

www.theintersection.org

Sidebrow is a member of the Intersection Incubator, a program of
Intersection for the Arts (www.theintersection.org) providing fiscal
sponsorship, networking, and consulting for artists. Contributions
to Sidebrow are tax-deductible to the extent allowed by law.

LETTERS TO KELLY CLARKSON

JULIA BLOCH

SIDEBROW BOOKS + 2012 + SAN FRANCISCO

What *is* the communal vision of poetry if you are curved, odd, indefinite, irregular, feminine. I go in disguise.

—Susan Howe, *My Emily Dickinson*

It was cool, but it was all pretend

—Kelly Clarkson, "Since U Been Gone"

Dear Kelly,

Lately I'm having that dream again, where there's an extra room I didn't know I had. It's a woman's dream, D. says. Last night my apartment unfolded an extra bedroom *and* an extra kitchen, and A. reclined on a futon in a Yankees baseball cap, glowering at me inexplicably. We were to serve dinner to twelve and thank god for the extra kitchen but it stretched very far away, tall and white. I wrought anxious over the cream-based soup, the way one is uselessly anxious in dreams.

Kelly I believed I could make it into something fine, make it fantastic. What will we do with these boys, these pretty tongues. Kelly you know how it is. You streak your hair & still it's the same morning every morning, and you're going for the eternal afterspank. It's nothing and sugar-colored coffee, it's don't you want me baby. Then you swell over the fact that you can name two affordable boarding houses in Paris, one across the street from the Gare de l'Est. Do you believe timing is everything?

Dear Kelly,

I feel it's time to wear more skirts, it's time to change brains, it's time to up my dose, it's time for less empathy. I don't have any appetite for this appetite. I tell my lover she's my little Hamlet when she cries and cries.

Let me explain: the feeling there's something else you're supposed to be doing is terrible as a flock of birds. I tried to up the antecedent. I was fit to burst with words. Honey, I wanted the hit.

Dear Kelly,

Love isn't always on time. Tonight you are more than automatic, you are full-bodied as treason, you are kiss-rated. Yeah. The strangest thing happened in Minnesota. I walked into the greenhouse I'd dreamt about. I swear. Messianic tile floor, alabaster fountain, abandoned card table. Right? You understand form, you shut down the bar. It's time to go global w/ this apocalyptic wish, *a moment like this*.

Dear Kelly,

Out near the freeway I confronted my extreme paperlessness. Woody and
entropic. Out near where we used to pick tomatoes off the road—the trucks
would swerve near dusk's steely sky, all lined up against one another like that
was the only way to be. We were just stopping. And you? And your oil fields?
This is the shirt of my intention.

Dear Kelly,

You know what gets me every time? The part where the piano jams at the chest. Where things go all lushy.

The intensity here is only getting intenser. The audience is armed, waving their nude wrists, ready to eliminate someone tonight. A great eye of public. But as G. says, what do they know about impulse-loving in the late nineties?

Dear Kelly,

It was utter words. It seethed. It was take another little piece of my heart, it was epic hair. I wanted the power to choose who was idol and who was dog.

Kelly it's almost time to go underground. We wrote our instructions in red on parchment along the rim of the parched day & the 'scape was dreamy & we thought we could fly we were 'bout ready to pop.

Dear Kelly,

Your lips are a caption, translating your perilous, wrecked face. Before the sparkly stage disappears you, you reverse the natural order. In which art + money = love. Your eyes are like flight; you can't get through a whole verse without crying over your dumb luck. I try to dignify myself on the pale couch, writing these notes down, but inside I abandon myself to the next huge dream. *In a moment you'll know who your idol is.* Girl you sure were swell up there, backlit and startling.

Dear Kelly,

Tell me I'm not pissing it all away as I wait for the phone to ring again. It's true, as you point out I wasn't really living. Earlier I noted that the cervix is nine-tenths of the law. She came along and I was fanatical, cocked, unseasonably warm. I was the revolving restaurant and she was the hotel. *Psych.*

Kelly I'm trying to do the right thing but there's a static in her voice fighting the urge to buckle. A fifteenth-century statue of Adam has shattered at the Met. Where does it end, this culture of guile? You are probable, sharp-edged. In the end, I'm going for the sensation.

Dear Kelly,

I feel the country of it, the way you starlet out on Leno, smashing your fine face up against the stage, laughing all the way to the big bank of cultural currency. In Pomona there is a place where you can gaze at a sky's dawning color above a pool of water that is deceptively deep, everything cut into a great square hold. A hole of air. I mean you cease to see the layers, I mean like the shape around the dress. You work basic black like something cold that is beautiful and getting colder.

Dear Kelly,

You know, sitting here, eating my microwaved tomatoes on somewhat tough toast, I think I could give myself another chance.

Seriously, can you tell me why I keep dreaming of a chipped white truck? Could it be the swerve of it, the handle? A rush of blood to the hand. Kelly I loved her like the painted flowers on concrete on Capp Street, which is to say tender and genuine and ornamental and, ultimately, uselessly. She really knew my stops. I did the math; I paid attention to the way light moves across a room. In my dream, people dropped from the plane like luggage but I ended up alone, licking lightly at the exit's metal edge.

Dear Kelly,

The chicken I take home to my lover smells slightly metallic; it's hard to tell, but I'm running underneath this skirt. Things kept rising at the back of the room so I dropped off the grid; I closed up shop. The cat's hiding deep inside the broken wall and I envy her passionate, sloppy logic.

You unfold like well-oiled myth. *No regrets for Kelly.* You're dancing as fast as you can, turning analog into meta, and I can't do anything but count clockwise.

Dear Kelly,

We have driven eighty-six miles south and parked under the *R* in the Compaq Center parking lot to see you rise like machination in a cloud of innocuous smoke. Z. finds the clasp on the baseball caps flimsy and I bitch about the price of soda but tiny girls' voices scream your name at the roof of the stadium and Kelly we love to love you.

I wanted to stop the world; I wanted to camisole out of this town; my thoughts turned to an elliptical machine for the brain. We could crush you with our fingers at this height. *San Jose, do you like to party?* Behind my father's house is a row of threadbare trees that I used to think made a forest. I've worn a pink skirt and tricked my hair in your honor. You are a love machine and you don't work for nobody but us.

Dear Kelly,

Then I'm east to get manicured on Main Street for this Byzantine wedding, is it dark enough to match my dress, can you blow-dry my hair for twenty dollars. Here is where I played in the orchestra for the caramel-colored assembly, damp chords of the celesta in *Carmina Burana*, just fit it in among the strings, oh yeah.

Finis origine pendet. But it's dry here, even the big wet snow is dry, I was crazy to run through it, it turned to hard, cold sunlight.

Dear Kelly,

The woman next to me on the plane jams her thumb against the clasp of her purse, trying to close it, her hand skids on the leather, *Oh sorry*, the way women apologize for their effort. I mean, she didn't even touch anybody. There's a map made of lights under the wing. I turn my neck and try to sleep on my horrible little pillow.

I call my lover from O'Hare's ruined dream tunnel with the neon fires. Kelly, I don't want that violin swell to overtake me.

Dear Kelly,

In Madison, Wisconsin, there is an office building called the Sonic Foundry. Can you tell me again about the curved bar, how she remembered the sound of my voice and followed me home before my hands filled with feathers?

Tonight you are a caged predilection. The eyes announce the face—I think this kind of attention is called *precog*. We wait and see.

Dear Kelly,

There are men on the scaffolding outside my office window wearing visors, goggles, and name tags that read VISITOR. Not everything can be cited, or hugged by steel. I am just subletting this job.

Later, on the 22 Fillmore, a woman with tremendous breasts bursting against black fabric fills her whole book with her face and I think of K. in the taxi outside the pink house. The accent on this bus, with its scopic audience, makes it hard to see the museum. Or maybe it's my own accident.

I drew it up in clay in my dream, comforted it with sawdust, all the long etcetera. Where is it, between what bridge. I want those panicked paintings. This city is one big collection of dissociated hands.

Dear Kelly,

O fabulous starlet, O freight of sound. A washed-out, harmless text shoals up the wall of the historical society, varnished to match fall's color. I know I can stomach a cramp like the next one. Now that I know what it's like to deserve new clothes, I can remember her kisses' throw-like disciplinarity. This season everyone's hunched over in their own private airplane seats, sight-reading the street.

Dear Kelly,

If I were to write blatantly, I would abandon explication: the shrunken skirt with the cherries pattern, the up-and-down motion while jogging, which resembles nothing less ordinary than a sad little breathing machine. I can throw all the lines I want from my hip, but there's not enough to string her up, even w/ the gourmet earrings and the eleven new leaves like clouds of green vapor outside the MUNI stop. What is the opposite of a drum?

Dear Kelly,

The hill behind my house smells of fennel and in my sleep I sometimes see the sun rise. Maybe the image is finite. Maybe every decision is photographed. When they go home from the bar she says *You make me feel like a porn star*—she'd always wanted to play like that, a Victrola in the background like a fringed skirt, like a filmed scene. Sometimes we cave into dream or fact, and sometimes we lack a theme song.

Dear Kelly,

And then, just like that, I'm watching the wave's jaw narrate my personal sense of manifest destiny. I mean, in the dream, the water came to the porch and I opened my mouth and blew out a little striped fish. R. remained calm, it being her farmhouse, she and P. being universally loved like thieves.

East again. And anyway in real time I danced alone w/ the baby at the wedding. In Virginia I went forth into the creek and into the abandoned red caboose with the rusted woodstove: IF THIS IS GOOD PLEASE TELL OTHERS ABOUT IT. We thought hard about why heat moves metal. In the morning the damp baby rolled onto my chest like a big cat. See? I'm every woman; it's all in me.

I dreamt that her number leapt up at me from the phone's face, a seething sort of vector.

Dear Kelly,

I'd like to go to Guatemala at all, T. remarked on our way back to the airport. She's always had an enormous soul. Driving pre-snow, I thought of the story about the oak tree that filled with fireflies before it buckled and wept at the horizon.

Kelly, what happened to January? I was deeply into Persephone, drinking a lot of Diet Coke.

Dear Kelly,

It's true: I don't know what it's like to be a victim of perpetual thinking, unable to pursue its end. I hear it's as sad and inevitable as a shopkeeper peering out of an empty Baccarat shop, as a NO SMOKING sign half in French, as the elliptical machine or a story about a word. But surely a thought can break open midair, like an airplane.

Dear Kelly,

Nothing's neutral, not the atmosphere's power to cool and soften, not skyscrapers, not the glitter embedded in sidewalks, not the violin's swell, the tug of the piano, that lush *At last*—it's a system and you are its fabulous, winged drone. I wanted a fashionable new tilt at the heel, an excuse to part my knees and let the black fabric dip. You wanted it, too, but then, I believe you're wholesome in the same way I believe the United States is a democracy, which is to say in a manner innocently misled.

.

Dear Kelly,

Sitting here today in a rainy café, waiting for my pocket to vibrate, I write to you in consideration of subjectivity. At the party I threw for myself I went from room to room clutching a plastic cup of red wine, worrying about my little sister trapped on the porch with an undesirable guest and watching my wrists move, clouded in black gauze. H. held me just a little too tightly as we danced but I guess that's not so bad, to be felt up at your own birthday party. It's hard not to take things personally, such as hot wind or a tow truck's resemblance to a crucifix. Sound in movement; space in sound; a connection to music that seems to be something acutely neurological.

Dear Kelly,

At London's Royal Academy of Arts we lurched past a mouth of death, a skirt of serpents, a Christ of feathers, a chest of feathers, a Lord of Death, a liver hanging like a bell or flower. I stood in a black wool skirt in front of a Viking burial scene, watching a ship set on fire & sent to sea.

Television is an event, too, but other times it's a curtain call, or it's fact masquerading as dream. What's it like, to be tiny? Does it hurt when I turn up the volume?

You mistake emptiness for innocence. This liver, suspended by hand, blooming, is also made of stone.

Dear Kelly,

Guess what? We got through March. Blossoms became seasonal. I wore black tights in England and split my knee open on Bernal Hill. We went to war. A vine grew behind the house with non-Minneapolis morning glories. And suddenly we wore May's artifice. Is your head a hat; is this your face and is it a flower; what is it like to prefer suggestion to definition; in other words, do you know what it feels like for a girl. That fusion of departure and memory keeps us here.

Dear Kelly,

The BART train pushes into 24th Street and I think about how cells are red, infrared, constantly dividing and then dying. C.'s death turns over and over, a sour/tart thing. To occupy the subway. K. in a dress the color of jaundice, rushing from the Oakland parking lot, her flat sandals going *slap slap slap* like a wronged wife, her gangly hands made to flinch in the late spring light. We're all just dodging cars on our way to the play.

Dear Kelly,

I wish this city summer were more like a Midwestern green envelope, more like a little wet mouth. Sunburnt trucks and the radio playing while some tough thoughts careen through your head.

Dear Kelly,

I can remember each sweaty crease in the bed. I was dreaming about my own body, but I answered my father when he asked me about ekphrasis. This is what it was often like. These are jobs. Like music is just a job. Sharp orange trees. Climbing a ladder, hanging around in a lot of vague light, having a personal pissing contest with the magazine in her lap.

Dear Kelly,

I envy your house burning down, a long, awkward, visible disaster. Like K. —
well, you already know about the little wings and the wedding dress, the
forced march and the mask. I dream about her, too: speedwalking through
the golf course at dawn, it seems anything could be new again. Then we go
running in Central Park and my heel turns, my nail chips, it gets dark and
I become the 'final girl,' sexy, sure, but doomed by unwashed hair and a
decent sense of color.

Dear Kelly,

The shoes I wear to the rehearsal dinner still have that new-car smell and I'm wearing red again at twilight when K. descends like one big white mouth. The guest to my left says the mural in the hall is *very New Deal*. Her collarbone like a pair of wings, the tendons of her arm like a child's chair, the grassy space where we cannot walk. What's it like, anyway, an open bar at the American dream?

Dear Kelly,

Envy and hunger move across the room toward me in a cheap blue rayon dress and last year's slingbacks. I want to wave my menstrual flag, curled like a new shell, but forego the hotel pool in favor of running to nowhere in this New Jersey. I follow a line of trees to the house as my sister asks what's the difference between *gray* and *grey*. We pass the sign that says 99¢ DREAMS and I say it's like *dove/pigeon*.

Later I search the fridge for some designer water for my ice and think of a boat at night, a cold knife, a zipper. I don't know what it's like to be part of a clan; no one in my family does. The next day at the airport I watch a girl rip her lettuce into small squares.

Dear Kelly,

Coming home, we cut diagonally across the city and sleep in a streetlit room where my lover makes a speech in her dream. I want to do an album of covers of famous poems, I said once, feeling attractively drunk. But choosing your friends is hard. In the morning the sun nearly slices the room open and we often wake panicked to butter-yellow curtains. Being bigger than you want to be means holding the body hostage while you complain about the 'now.'

Dear Kelly,

Because it was late July and I wanted to tell the crowd I was in my red period. Do you ever feel like one big ugly smirk? The morning layer of light had kept me at the edge of the dream, a light plying its own shadow on the wooden floor. Just this, you sing. *Just this*. Or a palm like a crushed cigarette, or being submerged in wet ice. I was really 'on' that night, someone said.

Dear Kelly,

I tell B. she's good at luck—for instance, this square of light hitting her palm. Sometimes a new lawn shoots up like a carpet of green stars and sometimes you get the mic for a full forty-five seconds. But c'mon, let's get competitive. I know you try your best to push the language, to demand more from a body. But the light covers you like an ulterior contract, a truly horrible song, this weather. Then the skin, nails, thigh, fringe of hair, though differently colored, are like a parataxis that rhymes with each commercial for a product we're all supposed to want simultaneously to bleach and fill us completely.

Dear Kelly,

It was unseasonably warm in the bedroom this morning when I re-read that good old poem about quite unnoticed Icarus falling through the corner of the painting. I am mixed up with you in an indexy way. Background music played wetly in the foreground as I received a phone call from the Temperance River in northern Minnesota. Turn up the volume: there's a wonderful sound hidden at the back of your voice, at the entrance to your throat.

Dear Kelly,

There is a new glass eye in the living room and we cook like we could ever eat enough. The body is really just another regular animal, like the way a running bra has handles. It's the angle, then the next angle, then the next throat. Little FOR RENT signs pinned up all over the city like prayer flags.

Dear Kelly,

If I have any agenda, it is one of desire. On television, we can see each curve of your skull; you live in a land of light gels and leg doubles, while meanwhile in our neighborhood the train has torn a groove in the road. Or, to be more specific, the body as a bright insect, without wings.

Dear Kelly,

Aboard the N line, which goes to either ocean, I think I might like to be a tennis pro and curve thru the chilled air. A star doubling as a star, you poke up at the Grammys slightly apoplexic, I mean, to blend in, but you'd rather be somewhere that's else. So I say baby if you want to eat it you should just eat it. Corners divide. Halloween makes everybody happy, and she's always dropping hints of herself into the poem until we realize we're renters in a town edged by sand.

Dear Kelly,

Torrid. One must always shoot a woman above the hip. These are rules that are spoken—I mean, embodied—as steam rises from the screen's heat, or shavings from a horse's hoof. I cannot pretend to dress like you any more; I am no Jennifer Jason Leigh and you are no eyestar.

In a mere four months we will elect our president, two whole seasons before the next plague of star jasmine.

Where is this exacting attitude of the arms?

Dear Kelly,

In Philadelphia, the trees stick their bare fingers up into the air. A cockroach climbs the step in my hotel room as CNN reads the names of the dead. Later we visit Whitman's narrow, unlit house; I push my hands down in my Haydnpockets; I eat fish aboard a boat and shimmy some in a red shirt against other bodies and really, I mean democracy they say got birthed here but it's just another cold city sometimes. And she gestures as a way to articulate the image inside her dress.

Dear Kelly,

Just another girl's mouth hanging open, arm wrapped around a painting, face flattened in a television show. When women run out of things to say, they turn to the weather. I drape a season across my days like a red curtain, try for a sweep. The anthems of a generation too saturated to absorb any natural light, one-note, high-note, brassy as a green lemon. Welcome to the desert of the real, as they say, begging silently for someone to take their fucking breath away.

Dear Kelly,

Clutched in femininity's dystopic embrace as if it were a big clammy hand from the deep, I watch the bright box, forgetting to blink, I know I should be turning to the book and reading and writing but the images keep coming, trafficking my sense of the real and the room. The screen is sometimes described as an eye or a tube filled with celebrity jelly. I can't see any of your pores; I know I shouldn't but I want you to be a real girl, muscular, with a hair shade that doesn't make a sound.

Dear Kelly,

Apropos of nothing, I wear the season like an animal's disguise, plan to wing it till the end of the year. There are many cords running across the length of the couch. Ideas coast in on ones and zeros, without color.

Dear Kelly,

In one letter, M. writes, *when inside is outside every organ is a messy eclipse*, and I feel that to be true, except on television. No visible organs, no pumping oxygenated red or blue. Just various colored waxes to affix to skin and I did not wear high heels until the age of twenty-seven. Because the battle isn't outside, I realized, as a thousand windows were shutting across the city.

Dear Kelly,

From high high up in the Opera House, I watch a woman's small dress bisect a glassy stage that reflects the snakey sea. O little ghost ship, O little curse—outside it's a grinning concrete day but in here we're underwater, gilded, impossibility gliding the space between brain and voice, a dark cloud of sound. *I think the industry could use a little class*, you once said. Tricked up on caffeine, I finger the difference on the page where your name turns from au courant into black and white. You're off somewhere taking your modernity leave, plotting a brand-new sound, or else grasping at threads as the curtain falls apart.

Dear Kelly,

Or Agamemnon's bright wound—I guess I forgot that we keep acting the story over and over. M. talks about *the unrelievable pressure an inside that wants to disrupt and slosh all over the sidewalk* & I'm in the Inner Sunset but my birthday's coming up in three days and I'm ready to hew to the new year. Ready to buy winter blackberries for 99¢ a box from the guy on the corner with the round face. Listen, the face is all there is.

Dear Kelly,

Miraculous, the shade on her fingers, the music streaming from the cord. A sensation of light on the thighs as we cross Market Street midday and something is running through the streets. Soon your voice will tunnel out of this city-town, welted and inconclusive. SOMA is filled with wind quartets: stop trying to make it happen and just let it happen. Soon you'll be flapping your great black feathers and ripping the roof off this whole experiment.

Dear Kelly,

This morning, the dream is balding, shedding its wings. On the stairs to nowhere I climb, reading my little magazine, pursuing my little life. Somewhere you're pressing your fingers into a plastic sheath and building a new memory out of pale clay while I clean the field of shining debris.

You'd like California. Fishes in water swell against the walls of the lake and the creek's a brighter green every time I go home for the holidays.

Dear Kelly,

Inauguration Day and it's like, I want to cash in the next season now, please. O your sophomore album, late and yet too soon. A girl drinking from a lake. You wear a cold jewel. I am in Pac Heights, in a black chair at Tully's. You'll still recognize me through the darkening window by the glittering at my breast. I know your voice has more to say—listen, everyone wants music that transports them, *Give me this moment* in the Tully's, like an arpeggio, I admit! I *love* Gershwin! The world, stinking blonde in its ordinariness, will take your face and make it simply your own. And in a distancing gesture she creates space around the memory.

Dear Kelly,

On the Amtrak, which passes each power plant between the valley and the coast, I watch this carpet of dark, flung low. I think of how you starlet out, make 'em swoony with their earnest slices of cardboard all glittered up with your name. As I ready myself to head off to my own little inner sunset, it's hard to remember anything could ever go out of style.

And sure, these flickers of yellow and green light that cast lines on the water are hopeful, like a miniskirt. Like your fold-out liner notes, italic and barren.

But things are more episodic these days. My lover gave me a ring set with green sea glass, and I think those lights could be stars.

Dear Kelly,

Astigmatism: my eye jumps to the next line, creating an 'imperfect image.' But corrective lenses make me homesick. A lot of wrong thoughts. And the new crop of idols are a sea of sequins, shopping bags filled with shopping bags, your visage reeling. Something receding. On screen again, are you bleeding from the hand or are you bleeding with the hand. I'd like a perpetual fork of white frosting to go with that 30-year-old discontent.

Dear Kelly,

K. came to my door in a pink skirt and a pink jacket, both the color of dust.
She opened her mouth and some dust came out. I am not totally sure what
happened between the foyer and the apartment door, I am stammering,
I did the treadmill for 35 minutes. Her legs stuck out of her skirt and she
murmured a lot, and almost cried, but did not cry one bit.

Dear Kelly,

Vegas is all light. But the electric kind, which casts a shadow. You know; I saw you touch your hand to your thigh. The *flap flap flap* of paper wings, call-girl flyers, a breast in your hand. And more light, cascading from the concrete to the sky. Stars are made here. Stars die here. It's the most revolving city I've ever been to. In the Watsu pool, I curl in her arms to tinny little music.

Dear Kelly,

All these weddings and their impulse toward the mirror. Sex like a collision we know we should avoid; wedding as XXX. Do you ever hate being American, flying Virgin, loving the master? I wander the aisles at Ross in search of a red blouse that ties up at the back. I'm thinking of the hushed motion, the crawl, the dark eye in the answer, the field of light around her palm.

Dear Kelly,

Unpacking again to a memory of a face. The stench of a new roof on our street overtakes me — time to break the cells of the city again. A green spot on memory. On the Great Highway piles of shit, beer bottles, new growth. Relentlessness of time, blah, blah, blah. It's May but the sky is still sweating, long past the season that is supposed to end all that. Where are your eyes now.

Dear Kelly,

I hear you've parted your hair a new way for the music video. I myself am dividing tasks according to what can be completed in front of the television, the depressive's gesticulations toward order. On my complaint letter to the airlines, my *sincerely* has been upgraded to *best wishes*—the twitching rabbit of ordinary brutality. Small bones, you say. Still, you must protect your throat from the hawks that can swoop down like the next big lie.

Dear Kelly,

At the piano recital, I hear the Yamaha sing out its cheap thick notes, the trick of wide keys' spreading their legs. I want to think you're grander than that, not coated in black gloss so shiny I can see the piano's pores flex and extend. A flat tone, too, not muted but—gagged. No. Not like that. I couldn't think where I was supposed to put my hands to make it better.

Dear Kelly,

I hear the anxiety air hourly. A fractured wind, a careening bridge, and then a stack of twigs, a bird fussing at it, outside my window. On the road from D.C. to Philly, the cars went all jittery. Everything pitched so high at first—the light glancing off fog, the empty cupboard, the concrete. The air conditioner crammed into my window spins all night. I drink beer and listen to your tinny voice on a small speaker.

Dear Kelly,

At a cold blue table a horn pinches at the air, its leads, its gestures. I didn't want to depart from the recording but my lungs had started to feel the effects of television's unfinished repair. Like my sister's face on the flute, that greenery, suburban pointillism, I'm not even sure you can read music. I am so tired of pointing, just pointing.

Dear Kelly,

The propellers chew air? And what kind of new clothes do I deserve? Ugh, what a repetitive gesture. You're here, somewhere, on one of the rows of city. Or you're not. The seats are small. I am sitting in a one-seat row opposite a woman with no bulkhead. The artificial speed grinds at the cells' native knowledge of movement. E., dropping into the water like a bullet. Sea, air, land. War hell, etc.

They say you've 'parted ways' with your 2002 image. If you look on IMDB you'll see some people like your ass but not your face. This puts me in such a despondency I know now how I want the book to end: on a crease.

Dear Kelly,

At the Aveda salon a flock of frosted tips worries the whole shelf of us, perched on perfumed naugahyde. This *Marie Claire* smears a small humiliation on the edge of my knee where I spilled my soy latte walking past the architectural receptionist. This morning, the cat left a line of vomit glistening on the wooden floor down the hall from my bedroom. At night, the wind clutches at the studio door. I am here to be beautiful, as according to the purposeful signs.

Dear Kelly,

There's a beautifully glassy surface around the compartment that is now slowly creasing. My lungs heavy with winter. There should be music playing out of my throat like smoke, some trumpeted, arrested moment. In the dream was this long suspended thing, a blue moment with high walls. Two faces. Green energy. Language coded because not totally seen. Tangentially, when I woke it was to terrestrial sunlight.

Dear Kelly,

Here, listening to Kansas City, its season of trumpets, I remember the side of her face in the alley outside the bar. I didn't want her to go, I wanted to hear more about her errant wife. The alto saxophone sculpts the air around the room, punches up the lights in bright wintry shades. You might see it as a candy-colored DNA model but the notes are harder than that, more forward, winging in unpurchased motion. Do you remember singing in the dry county, being born in a town saddled by the burden of its worth?

Dear Kelly,

Did I burn the letter, did I sleep with the T-shirt, did I wear the glass earring. My missing novel, my starlet with a feigned story in her mouth. My stolen subject lines, my oxygenated dress, my *light made lighter*, your aesthetic of the shitty. Pull it all down — you're not uncovering a new Greek god, the letters are not mammals, they do not talk. K. is gone, they moved to the suburbs and we are all here with the lights out.

Dear Kelly,

Stockholm blows from its diaphragms. Television again this morning. Sun breaking through window. One down, one up. Not yet a season, a pretend mouth of time with dry weather. You don't know, you've never come off the rail. The sky looks pathetic, worn out with time. Even the birds fall against it. At 20th and South a man stands with a perpetual shopping bag, peering at the cars. I smile when I leave the bus, his eye jolts through me. And yet I cannot quit this paper yet.

Dear Kelly,

Minnesota mouthfeel. I love everything here but everything's here stuck behind a screen and I can feel my breastbone creak under the weight. This morning in the new gymnasium I felt that there's a face near the center of my spine green with insect wings and chemically enhanced grasslings. North was tight snow. A thin bedspread locked with fever. On the elliptical machine my molars glance off each other as my calves pitch up and down and I read a story about a bird with its eye shot out.

Dear Kelly,

The minister tells me he doesn't think I have anything interesting to tell him as the room slowly fills with cherries and atmospheric liquid. It's like too-tight clothes in a cafeteria, a panic that scatters like rebar. It seems my fall is a long collection of these moments designed to plan the afterparty of my undoing. You have scored an 84 for Personality & Talent, a 75 for Sexiness, an 80 for Accomplishments & Fame, a 73 for Natural Beauty, and a 74 for Personal Style, resulting in an overall rating of 77 on AskMen.com.

Dear Kelly,

If I shut the breath, there will never be another Marx question I can't answer. The café is a good place to notice lesser wonders, like the way chair interrupts skirt. You and I both seem to have a hard time sometimes being with people. Still, now that I am old enough to phone my injured parents, to sit on a snowy runway and get that grainy feeling, I think that it might be time to return to technicalities.

Dear Kelly,

Broke the tip of the green fluorite on my way to retrieve some keys. Locked the sound within the cabinet. Had meringue for supper. Entertained a low feeling about sociality. Wore the skirt stained with fish sauce as I read the word *unicorn* as an adjective. Picked up a broken jar, slight wiry things, soiled cloth. Your old area code, my old area code. I am tired of trains, the cellphone alarm, coins, which words to run together and which to leave apart—so I broke the fall into four stages marked by red lines. I have it memorized in my hands, not my mind.

Dear Kelly,

I walked across the park and saw a tree burst. I shot things with the camera. The roses off MLK Drive were fearful. One moment was merely collected with the next and when you burnish gold, it looks like brass, but the bus fare hadn't gone up yet within the city limits. The next morning, I bought a necklace with a fingerprint in the silver, I suppose because I must have liked the idea of holding hands with my own neck.

Dear Kelly,

It is fair to be crossing, to have crossed. A face spinning, sculptural; broken grasses; wooden legs, small panacea and lucky for us. A day of dripping things. Elbow angled on bridge. What gets squared off in the park and what crosses the street to the museum. Then there is no promise in the other. I was sinking on the lawn, year after year. Your lucky face. And then it got very cool.

Dear Kelly,

This is not my first attempt at memory. For example, the two German shepherds in Orinda, my toy violin behind my father's real violin, a lesson about when to go swimming in the cold. The floor is designed to house us from the ground, but it is applied to the ceiling of a room, in its relation to the apartment above. Think in terms of Penelope's object and a floor littered at our feet.

Dear Kelly,

That night, I heard steps at the ceiling as the TV blinked its great blue eye and I thought of Penelope's great lack, not in terms of the object but the subject. Meanwhile we've lost the ground: ours is covered in soot from the landlord's garage which is hurled against our east wall. Soon the bed will outgrow the floor. Can you see the wood in pieces at your feet after the next big quake, a stormlike beating in dry heat, a city trying to behave like a desert under the weight of its own false liquids?

Dear Kelly,

Now that I know Sagittarius is my north node I have spent the day reading lines in an art gallery, trying to let my brain crawl into them or at least under some pastoral light. I think I should like to be erased, like a certain word is from these letters. No: I think I'd like to hold a certain feeling like a cut thing, with the light shining all around your forehead and the last failed year toppled over at the entrance to 101 on Bayshore. There was a sign there, and a view of the hill.

Dear Kelly,

I thought I smelled snow but it was just another dirty little cloud of burst gingko. If eye level is about five feet then how high is skin level. My mouth is working itself (again) and I remember that car in the air at the entrance to 101. I think these kinds of memories are called *peremptory*. I want to be a hoarder of empty spaces.

Dear Kelly,

Does mascara alter vision, in different degrees, according to its shades in blue or black? A memory of mostly banal driving, down Third Street and over to César Chávez, past Bayshore and the baseball diamond filled with mud and the cheap old Olympian. As if the hands were under water before filling with a number of thin things, metal wires mostly, bought from the painter who lives out near Ocean Beach in the sublet with the live iguana. The N broke down that night so we all crossed the Sunset in long glum steps. Out there the streets mechanistically rise and fall until you reach the sea. The magnolias were just starting to split open in January, and then I felt my hands coming through my face like cloth.

Dear Kelly,

We became obsessed with wires of silver that could be wrapped around our fingers. We booked our reservation. We saw threads. And glass filled with water—and a cloud around our own heads, jittery like ringtones. In Boston, we worked at getting our ice legs back. The hotel broke. So many enjambed hands and hours. Then it was March and the changing of the season was less like a fact and more like a wall wrap.

Dear Kelly,

Sweater instead of fear. Eyeliner instead of reassurance. Cocktail as cough suppressant, real men in real bar, I mean a bar cut like a man, I mean a bar cut like a piano, cut to fit around the piano, I mean a bar cut like a Yamaha baby grand, and a glossy drink, and your lacquered face, and instead of *anaphora* I said *anathema*, and the piano lodged under plexiglass like a big sideways fish and beneath the mirror is my coat check, is the cusp of your hand, is a mouth moving across the T-shirt. Long lines of the sun instead of the wrong side of the bed, in the bed instead of on the floor, I mean, in the bed but not in the bed, at the corner of the mouth, mouth across the T-shirt, and there is no narrow sleep before the portrait of your imaginary wife, so I moved to the other side of the bed and then the other side of the apartment and then from the second floor to the ground floor, I mean the ground, I mean the sidewalk where no one was wearing any costumes and the cab filled quickly with smoke.

Dear Kelly,

The runners on the Schuylkill locked in their corridors pass bits of molded white plastic that carve up the winter air. Garbage cars on the tracks, the absence of ice, all the city steps I have taken in my foolishly sensible shoes. I can spell words on paper. You think that's all the work you need to do, but you are not yourself, you are not this futurity. When I played in the evening I was sore in les yeux.

Dear Kelly,

I was moving one square of air from one corner of the country to another,
I held that square in my mouth or cheek so I could still talk, breathe, even
sing while holding it. I slept with it in my mouth, so even my dreams had
that square of air in them. And in the shower, and while running and
coffee and taking the bus. Once in a while if the bus jerked forward the
square would shift forward or to the other side, across my tongue. I tried
to keep my jaw very level with the square although I knew this probably
wasn't necessary, but it gave me a certain comfort to imagine the square
in abeyance. It was more difficult to hold the square in my mouth in some
countries than in others, not because of anything inherent about those
countries but because of the manner I assumed within them. On long
plane rides, while changing currency, on a new transit system the square
might tilt and with it my head.

SELECTED NOTES

page 16

after "I call'd the pangs of disappointed love / And all the long Etcetera of such thought": William Wordsworth, *The Prelude*

page 19

"every decision is photographed": Stephanie Young, "Resident"

page 24

after "Her connection to music seemed to be something acutely neurological"; "'There's sound in movement,' she says, and space in sound": Joan Acocella describing Suzanne Farrell in *The New Yorker*

page 25

after "He mistook emptiness for innocence, and paid for it": Adam Gopnick describing Joseph Cornell in *The New Yorker*

page 26

after "Even when she mastered the physics and geometry of taking an impeccable image, she preferred suggestion to definition": Judith Thurman on Julia Margaret Cameron in *Cleopatra's Nose: 39 Varieties of Desire*

page 36

after "a splash quite unnoticed / this was / Icarus drowning": William Carlos Williams, "Landscape with the Fall of Icarus"; after "he seems so mixed up with the Count in an indexy kind of way that I am afraid of doing anything wrong by helping his fads": Dr. Seward in Bram Stoker's *Dracula*

page 41

after "I push down my hands in my Haydnpockets": Tomas Tranströmer, "Allegro"

page 42

"Welcome to the desert of the real": Slavoj Žižek/*The Matrix*

pages 45 & 47

"when inside is outside every organ is a messy eclipse"; "the unrelievable pressure an inside that wants to disrupt and slosh all over the sidewalk": Dodie Bellamy, *The Letters of Mina Harker*

page 48

"A sensation of light on the thighs": Lyn Hejinian, *Sight*

page 65

after "Sir, said she, with a feign'd Story in her Mouth": Delarivier Manley, *Queen Zarah*

page 66

"And yet I cannot quit this paper yet": *The Weekly Amusement*, March 29, 1735

page 72

"It is fair to be crossing, to have crossed"; "small panacea and lucky for us"; "Then there is no promise in the other"; "And then it got very cool": John Ashbery, Irene Hixon Whitney Bridge, Minneapolis

page 78

"so many enjambed hands and hours": Bob Perelman, *Face Value*

page 80

after "I was popular, and I was lovely, and I played beautifully, and looked beautiful. But when I played in the evening I was sore in les yeux. Bonjour tristesse": David Helfgott to Michael Church in *The Independent*

ACKNOWLEDGMENTS

Some of the poems in this collection, some in previous versions, have appeared in the following publications and are reproduced with thanks: *Bay Poetics* (Faux Press), *Bird Dog*, *Cue*, *Double Room*, *Elective Affinities*: *Cooperative Anthology of Contemporary U.S. Poetry*, *Five Fingers Review*, the chapbook *Letters to Kelly Clarkson* (Mifflin Street Press), *The Letters Project* (15th Room Press), *O.NandOn Screen*, *P-Queue*, *Shampoo*, *Sidebrow*, and *Suspect Thoughts: A Journal of Subversive Writing*.

I am grateful to the following people, who were among those who helped me complete this manuscript with feedback, criticism, and encouragement: Dodie Bellamy, Kevin Killian, Zak Szymanski, Andrea Lawlor, Mattilda Bernstein Sycamore, Jan Richman, Drew Cushing, Ron Palmer, Kim DaSilva, Donal Mosher, Stephanie Young, Julian Brolaski, Cynthia Sailers, Erin Gautsche, Sarah Dowling, Janet Neigh, Barbara Joan Tiger Bass, and Allison Harris.

Julia Bloch grew up in Northern California and Sydney, Australia. She is the recipient of the San Francisco Foundation's Joseph Henry Jackson Literary Award and the William Carlos Williams Prize for Poetry, and she has published three chapbooks, as well as essays and reviews in *Journal of Modern Literature*, *P-Queue*, and elsewhere. She is an editor of *Jacket2* and lives in Southern California, where she teaches literature at the Bard College MAT program.

SIDEBROW BOOKS | www.sidebrow.net

SIDEBROW 01 ANTHOLOGY

A multi-threaded, collaborative narrative, featuring work by
65 writers of innovative poetry and prose

SB001 | ISBN: 0-9814975-0-0 | DECEMBER 2008

ON WONDERLAND & WASTE

Sandy Florian
Collages by Alexis Anne Mackenzie

SB002 | ISBN: 0-9814975-1-9 | APRIL 2010

SELENOGRAPHY

Joshua Marie Wilkinson
Polaroids by Tim Rutili

SB003 | ISBN: 0-9814975-2-7 | APRIL 2010

CITY

Featuring work from The City Project by Tyler Flynn Dorholt,
Danielle Dutton, Matt Hart, and Shane Michalik

SB004 | ISBN: 0-9814975-3-5 | DECEMBER 2010

NONE OF THIS IS REAL

Miranda Mellis

SB005 | ISBN: 0-9814975-4-3 | MARCH 2012

WHITE HORSE

A collaborative narrative culled from the White Horse project
and beyond, featuring poetry and prose by 25 writers

SB006 | ISBN: 0-9814975-5-1 | MARCH 2012

To order, and to view information on new and forthcoming titles,
visit www.sidebrow.net/books.